Fairies, Dragons and Unicorns

Illustrated by Molly Harrison

Featuring 20 fantasy art illustrations for you
to color! Great for kids and adults!

© Molly Harrison 2015 All Rights Reserved

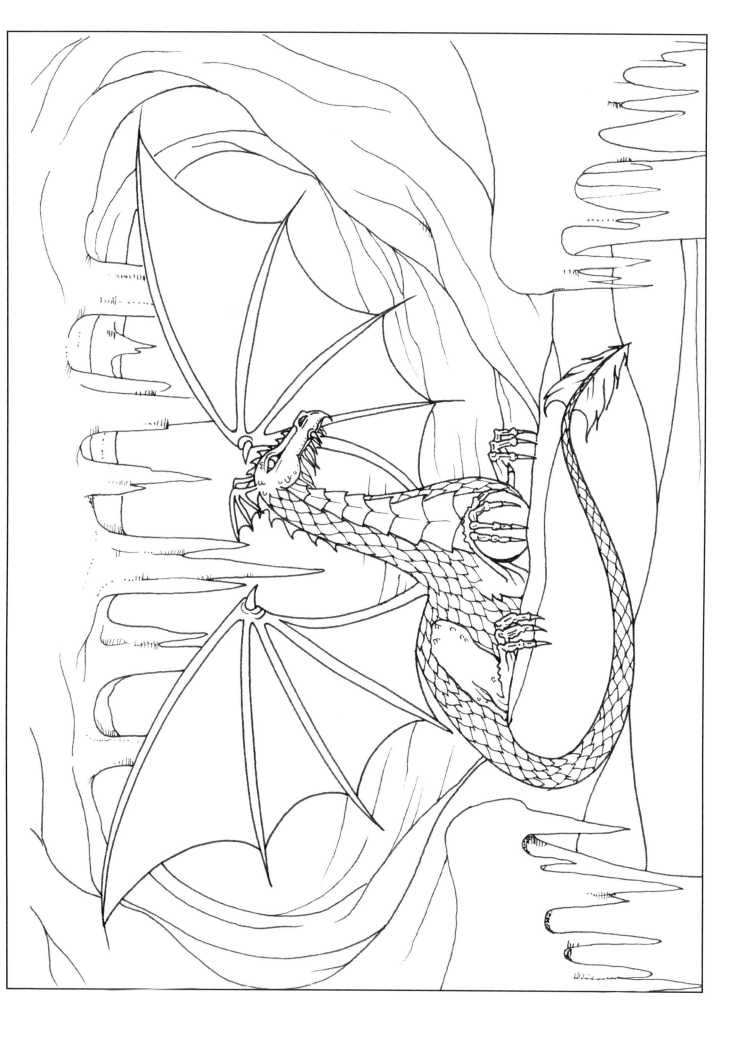

29100427R00025

Made in the USA
San Bernardino, CA
13 January 2016